Poetic Creations

by James Springer

James Springer

PAGE PUBLISHING
Conneaut Lake, PA

First originally published by Page Publishing 2024

ISBN 979-8-89157-783-1 (pbk)
ISBN 979-8-89157-800-5 (digital)

Printed in the United States of America

There have been a lot of poets:
Longfellow, Whitman, Frost and Poe.
But now it is my turn, so here we go!

I Only Wish That I Could Fly

Sitting on my roof, looking up at the sky
I only wish that I could fly.

To soar through the air, like a bird so high
I only wish that I could fly.

To leap from the earth, and say, "Bye, bye"
I only wish that I could fly.

I'd soar across the sea in the blink of an eye
I only wish that I could fly.

To land on a ship to the captain say, "Aye"
I only wish that I could fly.

I would glide for miles, without a sigh
I only wish that I could fly.

I jumped off the roof to give it a try
and to my wonder, I began to fly!

So always have faith in whatever you try
and maybe someday, you too can fly.

The Finding of the Grail

We went to a party at the county jail,
and they were looking for the Holy Grail.

Prison man was there, and he began to wail,
Spider Murphy has made his bail!

Now the Holy Grail is simply a cup,
And the doggy in the window wasn't a pup.

Bobby Darin was takin' a bath,
And Henry Fonda was doin' *Grapes of Wrath*.

The fat man on the hill thought it was a thrill,
But Mr. Peck said, "No," it was a mockingbird trill.

Humphrey and Katharine were ridin' on the Queen,
And the Everly Brothers were dreaming a dream.

Now the Grail is still hidden from the rest,
But Jack said, "No, it's to Cuckoo's Nest."

Off to the nest, we were running amok,
But the Grail was not there, we seemed out of luck.

Someone said: "It's on the golf course,"
Where else would it be? Of course, of course!

Now Jim and Arnie played to a tie,
But the Grail was not found by the by.

In the playoff, Arnie lost his gun,
Because Jim the Dink got a hole in one.

When they got to the green to find Jim's ball,
Chi Chi looked at Trevino and began to call.

The ball's in the cup, but it's made of gold,
Jim's shot had found the Grail, I am told.

So in the end, whatever we find,
We must always think of Gilda, who said: "Never, never, never mind!"

The Best Cowboy

Roy Rogers and his sidekick Gabby Hays
Were in the Westerns for days and days.

Then came Gene Autry, the singin' cowboy.
He was pretty good, but not as good as Roy.

Red Rider and Little Beaver, they were pretty good together.
They knew an Indian chief, his name was Red Feather.

The Lone Ranger and Tonto might have been the best.
But were they really, really better than the rest?

The Ranger's horse was named Silver, Tonto's was Scout.
They always caught the bad guys, there was never any doubt.

John Wayne was Rooster, a real tough guy.
His last name was Cogburn, who wore a patch on one eye.

Glen Ford was a storekeeper with very little drive.
No one in town knew that he was the fastest gun alive!

The Good, The Bad and The Ugly gave Clint a lot of fame.
And everyone knew "Eastwood" was his last name.

Matt Dillon was the Marshal of Dodge City.
He ruled the town and never showed pity!

Now these cowboys they all ruled the West.
But we all know John Wayne was really the best.

Life: Step by Step

Your mother and father put you one earth,
and your life begins when you are given birth.

You grow to become five or six.
Sometimes you played pickup sticks.

Eight years in elementary, then off to high school.
If you study hard, you won't be a fool.

Some go to college and some never will.
Many don't go cause they can't afford the bill.

Then you get a job and try to do your best.
You strive to be better, better than the rest.

Then you get married and for the kids you are glad.
Some grow up to be good, others grow to be bad.

Then your kids have kids along the way.
Now you're grandparents…what more can I say.

When you grow old, do it with a glow.
You look back on your life and say: "Where did it all go?"

When your life is over and you're about to pass,
You think to yourself: "It really went too fast!"

Androcles and the Lion

Caesar put him in the arena so the Lion could bring him to his end
But the Lion just laid down and became his friend.

The crowd wants blood, don't you see!
He just hugged the Lion and friends they would be.

Andy waved and waved and waved to the crowd.
He had a friend in the Lion of whom he was very proud.

The Lion roared and roared as loud as he could.
He hated the crowd like he knew he should.

The walls in the arena began to crumble.
The Lion kept roaring…he was not very humble.

People were falling and hitting the ground.
All they could hear was that deafening sound.

The Lion stopped roaring and rubbed against his friend.
They would stay together until the very end.

This Lion was one of a kind who had a good friend.
If your pet is a lion, you could come to a bitter end.

So if you want a pet, get a dog or a cat.
This story is now over, and that is that!

Moses

They say he climbed a mountain and was told ten things.
We should believe all ten no matter what life brings.

They're called "The Commandments" that we should live by.
We should all follow them, both you and I.

He was told to spread the Gospel throughout the earth.
He even told mothers after they had given birth.

They say he parted the sea to let people cross.
When I think about that I am really at a loss.

He was only a man who did the best he could.
He gave us guidance to live by, the way we should.

These ten things he told us about
are words we must covet and never have a doubt.

Now I'm pretty sure that he was real,
and this poem should tell you just how I feel.

So now I'll stop writing and close the door.
Because my mind is blank…just can't think anymore.

The Sun and I

I rise from my bed to begin the day.
I wonder what it will bring along the way.

I look to the east to watch the sun rise.
It happens every day, and that is no surprise.

It's a giant ball of fire that keeps us all warm.
I look up and say, "I'm glad that I was born."

The sun is a wonderment way up in the sky.
Without its heat, I know we would all die.

When it sets, we can see the moon.
It will rise again and very, very soon.

It crosses the sky from east to west.
When it sets once again, I will rest.

It rises and sets, and it happens each day.
I'm glad I'm here to see it; what more can I say?

The Sheriff and Me

I left Texas on a dark and sandy day.
The law thought I should be on my way.

An innocent affair with the Sheriff's wife,
Almost ended my young life.

I jumped in my truck and stepped on the gas.
He was comin' after me and comin' really fast!

I put her in gear and down the road I tore.
I was runnin' fast just like a razorback boar.

Him and his caddy were in hot pursuit.
Out his window, with his gun, he began to shoot.

Bullets were flyin'…flyin' past my head.
If he ever hit me, I'm sure I'd be dead.

I topped a hill and my truck took to the sky.
I never knew that my truck could fly.

Now he was gone, that mean old cuss.
He ran outta gas and had to wait for a bus.

THE MORAL:

The grass isn't always greener, so never take a chance.
Just keep your fly zipped and keep him in your pants.

For My Valentine

I was going to get a card for Valentine's day,
But I would rather do it in my own way.

Roses are red, violets are blue,
you are my Valentine and I love you.

Roses are red, violets are blue,
Everything I do, I do for you.

Roses are red, violets are blue,
Each day I think only of you!

Roses are red, violets are blue,
these are my thoughts, and this is true.

Roses are red, violets are blue,
You're my red rose and blue violet too!

A Picture of You

I raised my arms and looked to the sky,
I just did it, I don't know why.

As I gazed deep into the blue,
I saw a picture, a picture of you.

The one I've loved, right from the start,
and I'll love you forever and never part.

I don't know what's up there, deep in the sky,
and I hope I find out the day that I die.

I don't know what the future will bring,
and to that hope, I will always cling.

The picture I saw, the picture of you,
told me my love will forever be true.

I love you, I love you, I love you, I do.

Our Garden

We planted a garden to watch things grow.
Some grow fast, others pretty slow.

First year we had broccoli, zucchini, and peas.
I like to dig in the dirt and get down on my knees.

We had some tomatoes, they were all very good.
We ended up with about forty, like I knew we would.

There were other veggies, with seed we did sow.
It is a lot of fun to watch things grow.

Peas were the ones we grew the best,
'Cause we got more, more than the rest.

I made a planter box where Nancy planted some flowers.
They have lasted and lasted for many, many hours.

We planted artichokes and pomegranates too.
They both did well, they just grew and grew.

The things in our garden, all do we eat.
I'm pretty sad that we never planted a beet.

Now this poem about our garden has come to a stop,
Because we always grew a pretty good crop.

A Poet

I've wrote a lot of poems, some I'm saving.
It's like Edger Allen, who penned "The Raven."

Sometimes I think that I'm going mad.
Don't know if it's good or really bad.

I'm pretty smart and have a quick mind.
I think I might be just one of a kind.

If that last phrase is really true,
That means I might be better than you.

Now if I'm not, I really don't care…
Because I don't have a cross to bear.

It sounds like I'm braggin', but I'm really not.
I just know who I am and what I have got.

People don't know the poems that I've phrased.
If they did, they just might be amazed!

Now this poem is over and ends my story.
And if it's all true, then I'll be in my glory.

Trees

Trees give us oxygen, and it keeps us alive,
Without it, we would never, never survive.

They give us fruit, with what we ingest,
Some like the green, I think the red is the best.

Redwoods are tall and grow very high,
Myth may tell us, they can reach the sky.

Palms are pretty, they bear figs and dates,
others grow coconuts, but they're not mates.

Cedars have an aroma, and smell just fine,
But they don't grow as tall as a pine.

There are many types that grow on our land,
and I think they are all really grand!

Flowers

Flowers are nice, red, yellow, or green.
They're all very pretty, you know what I mean.

Some like purple…I like red the best.
I like all the colors, all the rest.

Plant 'em in a pot or in the ground.
Some will last all year round.

They bring you joy, for that I know.
Just give them some water and watch them grow.

For birthdays and weddings, they make a nice gift.
No matter when you get 'em, they'll give you a lift.

If you get some that are colored yellow
I think they will make you feel pretty mellow.

Roses are red, violets are blue.
Flowers always say: "I love you!"

Music

Music is universal, throughout the land,
and most people think it really is grand.

Music as about love and glory,
almost all tell a story.

If you like country, you may shed a tear,
'cause most are about cryin' in your beer.

Some are about a love triangle,
others may take another angle.

Opera is great, if you get the lingo,
others say, I'd rather play bingo.

No matter what you like, or what kind of band
It's still universal, throughout the land.

Ending, Beginning, Winning

Every ending brings a new beginning.
Life is short, so make sure you're always winning.

Live each day like it may be your last,
But keep your memories of the days that have passed.

As the days go by, your body may grow old,
always think young and never be bold

Look ahead and plan the next day,
Who knows what may happen along the way.

No one can tell what the future has in store,
So always keep smiling, never be a bore.

And so ends my story about always winning,
because every ending brings a new beginning.

A Clothespin

Clothespins are made to hold clothes on the line.
They hold 'em and hold 'em and do just fine.

Some are made of plastic and some are made of wood.
They all do a good job like I knew they could.

They have a little spring that holds the clothes tight.
They hold the clothes and do it with all their might!

When they get old and don't work anymore,
Just go out and buy some, and buy 'em at the store.

Now if one breaks and cannot be fixed,
Cut it in little pieces and play pick-up sticks.

Another thing you can do if it's past its prime
Is just throw it away and put another one on the line!

Aliens

I firmly believe there are aliens in the sky,
I also believe they have only one eye.

If they have only one eye to see,
That means they can only see half of me.

I'm sure they speak in a foreign tongue,
The way babies did when they were young.

Their crafts are round and shaped like a disc,
If they ever land, I'll punch one with my fist.

Most people don't think that they are really there,
And if they ever invade, I will pull out my hair.

And if I ever meet one, I'm sure I'll say,
"Get back in your disc and just fly away!"

Some say I'm crazy to write these poems,
Would you believe it, I also believe in gnomes.

Bridges

To cross a bridge, there is usually a toll.
Because bridges are guarded by a troll.

A troll so small, as ugly as can be,
And most of them look just like me.

If you have no money and can't pay the toll,
You better shapeshift and become a troll.

To cross a bridge, to get to your destination,
You gotta pay the troll, they're not a fascination.

If they open the gate and let you pass,
When on the other side, flip 'em the bird and say:
"Kiss my ass!"

Animals

I am writing this poem and I hope some are funny.
I'm really glad that I'm not a bunny!

Dumbo was an elephant, with ears he could fly.
If I was an elephant, I know I would cry.

An alligator has big jaws that could bite you in half.
I know they can't smile and can't even laugh.

The lion is king of the jungle, so they say.
If I ever see one, I will just run away.

A tiger is an animal that eats only meat.
Humans are made of this so would be a big treat.

The buffalo is one we should really dread.
'Cause he could butt you really hard with his head.

Once I had a cat and gave her a name of Meg.
She would go in a box and never had to raise a leg.

Now I think this poem is kinda funny.
I am still glad I am not a bunny!

The Hole

She said she would die on the spot.
I said: "WAIT! I haven't dug the plot."

When I began diggin' the hole
I had to deviate because of a mole.

Now the hole is dug and ready for her to lay down,
But she's not dead yet, so I'll have to look around.

She's eighty-one and still very bold,
and she'll live a very long time, so I am told.

Now if she ever dies out of spite,
I will dig another hole and make it right.

If she is gone before my end,
I'll write on the head stone, "Here lies a friend."

The Computer

The computer is a tool, a tool of the ages.
If you wrote what it will do, it would take a million pages.

On the Internet, there are many things you can find.
When I think about it, it just blows my mind.

If you use it, it's really hard to gain perfection.
When most of us use it, we need a lot of direction.

No one knows all the things it can do.
Sometimes I just get lost, how about you?

You can send an email to all your friends.
If you use the phone, sometimes the conversation never ends.

It works on binary, that's ones and zeros…I'm sure you know
It can go on forever…it can just go and go!

It can make a robot do whatever you say.
I think I got lost somewhere along the way.

Hackers can hack in, they do it every day.
So when you use your computer, be cautious about what you say!

Wine

Wine is a drink that you can savor.
Smell the aroma and taste the flavor.

Open the bottle and remove the cap.
Drink too much and you'll need a nap.

Some prefer Cabernet Sauvignon.
Others just like to sip it when they're alone.

Wine is good for you, some people say.
Don't overdo it…keep it at bay.

Some like to drink it around suppertime.
I think they do it 'cause the taste is sublime.

Wine is a drink that has a good nectar.
When you drink it, drink from a scepter.

When you drink it, don't drink it too fast.
Just sip it and sip it…make it last.

So if you drink wine, do it with ease.
May I have another glass, please, please, please!

Beer

I drink Bud Lite 'cause I like it the best.
Now don't get me wrong, I do like the rest.

I keep it in the fridge, so I can keep it around.
I never drink too much, or I'd hit the ground.

I drink two or three and do it every day.
I do it because I like it…what more can I say?

Some people like Coke and Pepsi, I am told.
But I like beer, it's a little more bold.

Wine is 14.5 percent booze.
Beer is 4.2, that's what I choose.

Whatever you drink, it may bring you cheer.
Now I'm all done…gotta get another beer.

He Shoulda Used Red

Matt went to the Longbranch and walked in the door,
He was tall and lean and stood six foot four.

He sat at the bar and ordered a beer,
He said Kitty has left me, as he shed a tear.

She ran off with Chester,
Who looked like Uncle Fester.

He downed his beer and headed for the door,
And what he saw made his jaw hit the floor.

Someone had painted his horse blue,
He was really teed off, and this is so true.

He said, "I'll find out who did this deed,
And who had the guts to paint my steed?"

The Red Dog Saloon was not far away,
He saw drippings of blue paint that led the way.

He entered the Red Dog, mad as can be,
He saw blue paint on a man named Ski.

Bullets were flying, and Ski hit the floor,
Matt calmly turned and walked out of the door.

Back in the Longbranch, he knew Ski was dead,
He turned to Doc and said: "He shoulda used red!"

Doubt

I look to the sky and wonder, What's there?
Then I think to myself, do I really care?

No one really knows, what's beyond the blue,
Most think it's God, but is that true?

I don't believe in idols, but that's just me,
I would smite the golden calf and cast it to the sea.

They say he died to save our lack,
Just live day to day, never look back.

If you become sick, lying in bed,
I know you will wonder, "What lies ahead?"

When I think of these things, I have a doubt,
I hope when I die I will really find out.

From Now Till Then

I will never grow as old as a redwood tree.
I just wanna last and see how old I can be.

I've been around way past eighty-five.
I thank what's up there that I am still alive.

I've had some troubles along the way.
And now I just take it day to day.

I really don't know how long I'll last.
I hope to see tomorrow and forget the past.

When my time comes, I'll be pretty sad.
So far my life has been good, for which I'm glad.

I don't think about dying and that's very true.
I want to stay happy until I'm through.

This story is not quite over, one thing left to say.
I'm gonna play, play, till my daddy takes my T-bird away!

Time

When you get to be as old as me,
The best just maybe yet to be.

I think of all the things I've done,
Some were bad, but most were fun!

The memories I have are all like gold,
I'll remember each one, no matter how old.

Friends I've had along the way,
I think of them each and every day.

Time is beginning to wind on down,
I look upon it without a frown.

Growing old is not a crime,
It's a fact of life, you can't stop time.

The days go by, as in the past,
I wonder which one will be my last.

Seven Deadly Sins

1. Gluttony:
    Eat too much, get obese, and keep on eating.

2. Greed:
    Get rich and want more and more!

3. Sloth:
    Be lazy and have no motivation.

4. Envy:
    Want what others have that you do not have.

5. Wrath:
    Do evil to others and have no remorse.

6. Pride:
    Be yourself, trust who you are, and know it.

7. Lust:
    Gluttony, Greed, Sloth, Envy, Wrath, and Pride.

You should avoid these seven deadly sins I've written about.
Because none of them are good, there is no doubt!

There may be an exception to these seven things.
And that is Pride, just don't flaunt it whatever life brings.

So in the end, there is just one last thing to say.
Don't commit any of these seven sins, just keep them at bay!

Shoes

Shoes are items you wear on your feet
Some aren't very pretty, others look neat.

The back part is called the heel.
If they fit, oh, how good they will feel.

The middle part is called the arch.
They give you support even if you happen to march.

The front part is called the toe.
And that's where your little piggies go.

Men and women wear a different kind.
So many styles and that just blows my mind!

Men wear wing tips, oxfords, or loafers…don't you see.
I like slip-ons the best, but that is just me.

Women wear flats or heels, some five inches high.
There are many styles to choose from by the by.

So when you wear shoes, make sure they fit right.
Not too loose and never too tight!

Now there is just one thing left to say:
Don't buy too many, keep that urge at bay!

Our Flag

Our flag is the symbol of our land.
Most of us think that it's just grand.

It has fifty stars, one for each state.
I believe in what it stands for, and that is great!

It has some stripes, some red, some white.
And I will honor it with all my might.

On Iwo Jima, four soldiers raised Old Glory.
I am sure we all know that great story.

If someone of stature comes to their end,
It flies at half-staff to honor who has been.

If you are in peril and have some doubt,
Fly it upside down and someone will come to help out.

The flag is the symbol of what we stand for.
I will honor it until he knocks on my door.

Now there are some who don't think our flag is swell.
All I can say is you can go straight to Hell!

Dos and Don'ts

1. Follow my lead, as listed below.
2. Strive to do better than you think you can.
3. Always look twice because what is really there is not always revealed at first glance.
4. We all have an ego. Don't flaunt it!
5. Keep an open mind. Don't have tunnel vision.
6. While driving, if in doubt, DON'T!
7. Don't try to be something you're not.
8. Always try to be kind.
9. Have faith in yourself. Don't be negative.
10. Stand up for what you believe in.
11. Don't be an actor. Be who you are.
12. Don't exaggerate.
13. Think before you speak.
14. Be truthful. Don't lie.
15. When talking to others, consider the source.
16. Don't yell at others. Keep your cool.
17. Listen and you shall learn.
18. Look deep and you shall see.
19. If in danger, don't panic.
20. The grass isn't always greener on the other side.
21. If you don't have control, then don't worry about it.
22. Don't be a fool…keep your cool.
23. Don't be a bore.
24. When you learn—teach.
25. When you get—give.
26. If your words are not kind…be quiet.
27. When you love someone, tell them often.

28. Smile often, laugh loudly, and love deeply.
29. Do random acts of kindness often.
30. Forget me not, but if remembering becomes a task, then forget.

Famous Quotes

"Don't throw rocks."	Chaucer
"I feel your pain."	Clinton
"Frankly, I don't give a damn!"	Gable
"Go ahead, make my day!"	Eastwood
"Are you talkin' to me?"	DeNiro
"Ask not what you can do for your country…"	Kennedy
"Look, Ma, top of the world."	Cagney
"Failure to communicate."	Luke
"Read my lips…"	Bush
"Stella! Stella!"	Brando
"Make an offer you can't refuse."	Brando
"The jump will probably kill you!"	Newman
"If the shoe fits…"	Cinderella
"You can't fool Mother Nature."	Dietrich
"Float like a butterfly, sting like a bee."	Ali
"Good guys finish last."	Leo Durocher
"Here's looking at you, kid…"	Bogart
"Play it again, Sam."	Bogart
"The grass isn't always greener."	Ovid
"Don't throw rocks if you live in a glass house."	
"Nero fiddled while Rome burned."	Nero
"One small step for mankind…"	Armstrong
"The only thing we have to fear is fear itself."	Roosevelt
"A date that will live in infamy."	Roosevelt
"Ninety-nine and forty-four, 100 percent pure."	Ivory Soap
"Forget me not…but if remembering becomes a task, forget!"	Springer
"No more ink, no more pen, just can't think…amen!"	Springer

About the Author

James Martin Springer was born and raised in Portland, Oregon. He was musically inclined and took piano lessons for nine years. His passion for baseball developed and replaced the piano lessons. He graduated from Roosevelt High School and enlisted in the air force at age eighteen and stayed for twenty-two years as a missile guidance technician for ten years and then an air traffic controller for twelve years. He spent one year in Greenland, four years in Okinawa, and two years in Vietnam. James retired as a master sergeant.

He has two sons, three grandchildren, and three great grandchildren.

James is an avid bridge player, enjoys dancing and karaoke, and is an entertainer. He plays the piano and sings in two shows he has developed: "Memory Lane Music Review" and "Springer Magic." He continues his love of baseball.

He currently lives in Mesa, Arizona, and has written poetry for less than a year.